BRITAIN IN PICTURES
THE BRITISH PEOPLE IN PICTURES

BRITISH DOGS

GENERAL EDITOR
W. J. TURNER

BRITISH DOGS

A. CROXTON SMITH

WITH
8 PLATES IN COLOUR
AND
24 ILLUSTRATIONS IN
BLACK & WHITE

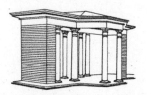

COLLINS · 14 ST. JAMES'S PLACE · LONDON
MCMXXXXV

PRODUCED BY
ADPRINT LIMITED LONDON

PRINTED IN GREAT BRITAIN BY
THE SUN ENGRAVING CO LTD LONDON AND WATFORD
ON MELLOTEX BOOK PAPER MADE
BY TULLIS RUSSELL & CO LTD MARKINCH SCOTLAND

LIST OF ILLUSTRATIONS

PLATES IN COLOUR

BLACK AND WHITE ILLUSTRATIONS

ROMAN TESSELATED PAVEMENT
Cirencester

DOGS OF THE DIM AGES

JUST when man and dog first formed the alliance that has proved so beneficial to both is a matter that is still conjectural, though the scientific gentlemen who unravel the secrets hidden in bones and stones are constantly enlarging our knowledge. We are not concerned here with the discoveries made in foreign countries, but must confine our survey to these islands. One thing is certain—our primitive forefathers who existed many thousands of years ago had their dogs, the earliest evidence of which, to the best of my knowledge, was disclosed in 1928 as Mr. A. Keiller and his associates were excavating at Windmill Hill, near Avebury in Wiltshire.

They then discovered the remains of six distinct domesticated dogs, those of one being sufficiently complete to permit the reconstruction of the skeleton. The depth at which it lay, enabled Mr. Keiller to assign it unhesitatingly to the Neolithic period, and the belief was expressed that in life it had been a combination of hunting and domestic animal. That period, though removed from us by some thousands of years, marked an important stage in the progress of mankind. Britain was then separated from the continent, but about 2000 B.C. we had an invasion by what were known as the "Beaker" people of the Bronze Age from Central and North-Western Europe, men who hunted, cultivated land and kept domestic animals. Did they bring dogs with them?

We have no evidence that dogs coeval with those of Windmill Hill survived. They may have done, but there are no traces of them among our modern *canidæ*, all of which seem to have come from overseas. In fact, it may be said that we have no really indigenous breeds, although a number have been with us long enough to enjoy all the benefits of naturalisation. Hundreds of years separate the "Beaker" folk from the landing of Julius Cæsar in 55 B.C., yet at some time or other Mastiffs were acclimatised by the Britons, and had

7

become so well established that the conquering Romans, impressed by their bulk and courage, exported them to Rome to fight in the arena. I think it is established that Mastiffs and other old breeds were of Asiatic derivation, and the remarkably vivid sculptures in the Assyrian rooms of the British Museum are enlightening, showing as they do huge dogs of the Mastiff type belonging to the reign of Assur-bani-pal (668 to 626 B.C.).

Two theories may be advanced to account for the presence of Mastiffs in ancient Britain. Phœnicians, in their quest for tin, may have brought them from the Eastern Mediterranean, or they may have been imported by way of Belgium. Strabo, the Greek geographer who was born in 63 B.C., complained that at times the Gauls had bought up their Mastiffs for use in the battlefield. A century or so after the advent of the Romans we had various breeds, which may have come with them or belonged to an anterior date. In a Stationery Office publication on Corbridge Roman Station we read that among the domestic animals disinterred, "dogs were numerous, and included [apparently] both Whippets and Dachshunds." This station in Northumberland was occupied by the Romans from before A.D. 80 until about A.D. 120 Quite possibly the "Whippets" were smallish Greyhounds, for they are a breed made last century from crosses between Greyhounds and one of the Terriers, possibly with the help of Italian Greyhounds. Mention of a Dachshund-like dog is interesting. The name, of course, is comparatively modern, but German scientists have written of short-legged, long-bodied dogs having been known for countless years under the generic term of Basset, in which they include Dachshunds, Basset Hounds, and the Terriers of that peculiar formation.

By the time of Alfred the Great (A.D. 871), we are sure there were dogs of several kinds in the country for Green, in his History, writes: "He passed from court and study to plan buildings and instruct craftsmen in gold-work, to teach even falconers and dog-keepers their business." We cannot guess what the dogs were, some of them may have been Greyhounds, which are thought to have come with the Celts in their westward migrations, one wave of which reached Britain before the Christian era. Alfred also made a law specifying the compensation to be paid to anyone bitten by a dog.

We have now left the dim ages and reached the time of the recorded word. In his work on *The Enclosure and Redistribution of our Land* Mr. W. H. R. Curtler has an informative note relating to the end of the tenth century: "Similar to the duties of these men (oxherds, cowherds, etc.) were those of the shepherd, *opilis*, who drove the flocks to their pasture, the scypham, where he guarded them from wolves with dogs." The dogs, one imagines, were those of a powerful frame that were needed as guards, not for herding, the like of which are still to be found in most countries of the continent. It was in this century, too, that Howel the Good (Hywel Dda), who ruled over South Wales, promulgated laws in which there are numerous references to dogs— big dun-coloured hounds, Greyhounds, Spaniels, smaller hounds that may have been Harriers, and Sheepdogs.

8

ANNE OF DENMARK AND HER GREYHOUNDS
Oil painting by Paul van Somer

LAND SPANIEL

Oil painting by George Stubbs, 1724—1806

FOR some centuries the Forest Laws were of immediate concern to certain classes of dogs and their owners. Harsh and oppressive in operation, they illustrated the vast gap that separated the monarch from his subjects, and after they had disappeared traces of them lingered on under the guise of the Game Laws. When a man desires to arrogate to himself privileges and pleasures it is not unusual for him to contend that he is doing so for the benefit of others. "The King having a continual Care for the Preservation of the Realm, and for the Peace and Quiet of his Subjects, he had therefore, amongst many Privileges, this Prerogative, *viz* To have his Places of Recreation wheresoever he would appoint."

So it came about that the first Forest Laws were drawn up by Canute. "Charta de Foresta, of Canutus, a Dane, and King of this Realm; granted at a Parliament holden at Winchester, Anno Dom. 1016." In one sense it may be said that these laws had an effect that was ameliorative. Before they were made, a man who killed any wild beasts in a forest was not punishable by law but at the will of the king, who might inflict upon him the loss of a limb or even of life. The Charta de Foresta did at least provide that no man should lose life or member for killing venison, that is for killing any beasts of forest or chase.

A little time ago I was fortunate enough to find a copy of Manwood's *Treatise of the Forest Laws*, which was first published in the reign of Elizabeth. This somewhat rare work, which is sometimes quoted incorrectly in books about dogs, is a mine of information on sporting customs, and it is now among my most prized possessions. Occasionally one comes across a definition of a word still in common use, that is not to be found in the dictionaries. "Before this Nation was replenished with Inhabitants, there were many great Woods full of all sorts of Wild Beasts then known in England." The growth of population brought about the destruction of these woods, but, even in Saxon times, many were not destroyed, "and those were called Wolds, that is, Forests or Woods where Wolves and Foxes did harbour." As the "ravenous Beasts" disappeared, there remained "Beasts of Pleasure, as well as delicate Meat," and these the kings sought to preserve for their own sport by the creation of forests.

According to Manwood "a Forest is a certain Territory of woody Grounds and fruitful Pastures, privileged for wild Beasts and Fowls of Forest, Chase and Warren, to rest and abide there in the safe Protection of the King, for his Delight and Pleasure; which Territory of Ground so privileged is meered and bounded with unremovable Marks, Meers and Boundaries." These delectable tracts of country were reserved for the enjoyment of the king and a few nobles who had his permission to hunt therein. If a man started his hounds on game of any sort outside a forest, and the animal crossed the boundary, then the hounds had to be called off by the blowing of a *Rechase* on a horn, and if they killed their owner was regarded as a trespasser and made himself liable to penalties, unless he could prove that he had done his best to prevent them.

"Hunting in Forests is Sport for Kings and Princes, and therefore not to be used by every common Person, but only by such of the Nobility and others who have Authority from the King or from his Justice in Eyre, or other Officers of the Forest." Ergo, common people could not be allowed to keep dogs, within the bounds of a forest, that were large enough to kill or disturb the game. Manwood has a whole chapter on this subject, which is prefaced by the explanation : "The Laws of the Forest do so much regard the necessary Use of Dogs, for the safety of Mens Goods and Houses who live within the Boundaries thereof, that certain Dogs are suffered to be kept therein by any Person whatsoever. But some Sorts are not suffered to be kept there, but only by particular Men."

Mastiffs being the most formidable guards of those times, every farmer and freeholder dwelling in a forest might keep one about his house, provided that it had been lawfully expeditated according to the laws of the forest. Expeditation, a clumsy word, came, we are told, from the Latin *expeditor*, to lame or make unable to run. It was a change for the worse from the *mutilatus* of Edward I. "In the 31st. Canon of Canutus, the lawing of Dogs is called Genuscissio, which was a cutting or laming them in the Hams; and therefore the old Foresters called it *Hamling* or *Hoxing*." The brutal custom of expeditating was introduced by Henry II. One shudders on reading Manwood's description of the process : "Three Claws of the Fore feet shall be cut off by the Skin : And accordingly the same is now used, by setting one of his Fore feet upon a piece of Wood eight inches thick, and a Foot square, and then setting a Chizel of two Inches broad upon the three Claws of his Fore foot, to strike them off at one Blow; and this is the manner of expeditating Mastiffs."

It does not seem to be altogether clear in the earliest Forest Laws that Mastiffs only had to undergo this disability, but custom at any rate excluded other breeds, even Greyhounds. Mastiffs, then, of course, were not the slow, heavy animals of the present day, but were obviously capable of chasing and pulling down a deer. Small dogs, "to look after things out of the Covert," were exempt, for they could do no harm, and consequently men were allowed to have them. I wish we could know what they were. Probably some of them were Spaniels. . . . "the Dogs which are allowed to be kept in the Forest, shall be such which are not able of themselves to hurt the Deer; or such which are disabled by the Law of the Forest." For some reason unexplained Greyhounds, too, were free from mutilation, "yet there is more danger in those Dogs than in Mastiffs. 'Tis true, Greyhounds and Spaniels are generally forbid, that is, they are not to be kept in a Forest, but only by a Grant from the King."

Every three years the dogs kept within the boundaries of a Forest had to be viewed by "twelve lawful Men, and not otherwise; and the View and

VARIOUS KINDS OF DOGS USED IN HUNTING
Illumination from *The Master of Game*, *c*. 1450

Enquiry being to be made by the Regarders of the Forest, who are twelve
lawful Men, sworn and appointed for that Purpose." A sort of rough justice
was observed in these proceedings. The Regarders had to be at pains to
ascertain the lawful owner of any dog that offended, and he alone was respon-
sible for the payment of the fine of 3s., except that any person who had been
entrusted with the charge of such a dog was liable. Should a man have two
Mastiffs that were not expeditated he was only fined for one, but if two men
were joint owners of one dog each had to pay the fine. Apparently, for some
offences, the fine was adjusted according to one's station in life. "If a Peer of
the Realm, or a Bishop, is presented for keeping such Dog, he shall pay only

3s., and not according to his Quality; but if a Peer is presented and indicted before the Justices of the Forest for keeping a Greyhound, and hunting with him there, in such Case he may be amerced by the said Justices according to his Dignity and Estate."

My edition of Manwood is the fourth, which was published in 1717 and revised by William Nelson, barrister-at-law. Although the substance was untouched, the orthography was modernised and certain additions made that carry the information to the days of Queen Anne. So we get particulars about Greyhounds to which reference will be made later on. In the course of time these restrictions upon dogs became a source of revenue to the Crown, owners being allowed to avoid having them mutilated by payment of fines. Others were exempt on account of services to the king. In the reign of Edward I "the foresters, regarders and other jurors of the New Forest say upon oath that the men of Lymmithorn (Lymington) are quit and ought to be of expeditating their dogs of the same town up to a certain number, to wit, thirty-two dogs." In A.D. 1270 the burgesses of Northampton received permission from the Crown to keep their dogs, both in the suburbs and in the town, without having them lawed. Nearly 200 years earlier the inhabitants of the county of Northamptonshire, as recorded in Domesday Book, had to render to the king forty-two pounds for dogs—that is to say, they had to pay for the support of the royal dogs four times the whole rental value arising from the town. Going back further still, it was stated that the same county had to find three thousand cakes of dogs' bread for Edward the Confessor. Northamptonshire is brought into the picture, not because it was in any way singular, but merely to serve as an example of what happened in the rest of the country.

Put bluntly, the kings largely took their pleasures at the expense of their subjects. In the reign of Henry III the sheriff of Northamptonshire was ordered to see that the royal huntsman, with two horses, three men and sixteen dogs should be taken care of for the purpose of running fallow deer, and a like number of men and horses with fifteen dogs for hunting stags. One Richard Basset paid five marks to King John for a licence to keep dogs to hunt fox and hare. Radulphus de Eyneston got himself locked up in Northampton Castle for taking Greyhounds through the royal forest without having them on a leash. So one might go on indefinitely, one county being very similar to others. Although the severity of the Forest Laws was relaxed to some extent under Magna Carta, they were by no means abolished at Runnymede, and when they fell into desuetude the Game Laws continued to deal harshly with the common people.

The barons and landed classes generally, who in the course of time were allowed to enjoy their sports untrammelled, clung tenaciously to their privileges, and at one time poaching was punishable by transportation. Solicitation for the moral welfare of the lower orders was often put forward as an excuse for prohibiting poaching. Thus, Professor G. M. Trevelyan in his fascinating book on *English Social History*, records that "In 1389 the Commons complained that 'artificers and labourers, and servants and grooms keep Grey-hounds and other dogs, and on the holy days, when good Christian people be at Church, hearing divine service, they go hunting in parks, warrens and coneyeries of lords and others, to the very great destruction of the same.'" As late as the first quarter of last century the Game Laws found justification in the plea that they were intended to prevent inferior tradesmen, apprentices and dissolute persons from leaving their proper occupations in pursuit of game, to the injury and ruin of themselves and families.

The Game Laws come within the scope of this book because one of the chief auxiliaries of the poacher is that clever rascal, the Lurcher, a compound of Sheepdog and Greyhound, with the brains of the one and the speed of the other. Many imagine that the term Lurcher is of comparatively modern derivation. It is as old as Queen Anne, and no doubt was in use before that queen. "He who keeps Greyhounds, Lurchers, Setting-Dogs, to kill the Game, being not qualified, forfeits £5, a Moiety to the Informer, the other to the Poor." So runs a statute of Queen Anne. If it were not for his dis-reputable associations the Lurcher might very well become a favourite com-panion on account of his cleverness and teachability. So much for the Forest Laws and their successors.

DUNNE HOUNDE
Woodcut from Turbervile's *Book of Hunting*, 1576

13

WE have seen that Greyhounds, Spaniels, Lurchers, Mastiffs and divers other dogs not mentioned by name appear in the Forest Laws, and that Sheepdogs of sorts were also in early England. Although Spaniels did not fall within the prohibitory clauses of these laws, we know that they were of moment to sportsmen, who used them either for the purpose of flushing game birds to the hawk or driving these birds into nets. When or how they came into England is not known, but it is commonly agreed that they were so named because they originated in Spain, probably reaching us through France. One of the earliest books on British sport is *The Master of Game*, which is mainly a translation of the French *Miroir de Phoebus*, by Gaston de Foix. Some ascribe the work to Edmund de Langley, first Duke of York and fifth son of Edward III; but the Shirley MS. attributes it to his son, Edward Plantagenet, second Duke of York. Possibly both had a hand in it. The attribution to Edmund is excusable, because, according to the *Dictionary of National Biography*, he was an easy-going man of pleasure, who had no care to be a lord of great worldly riches.

> "When all the lorders to councell and parlayment
> Went, he wolde to hunte and also to hawekyng."

It is not of much moment either way, the pertinent matter being that Spaniels and hawks come very much into the picture, as well as hounds. "Another maner of houndes ther is that byn clepid haundis for ye hauke, and Spaynels for ye nature of hem cometh from Spayne, notwithstondyng that ther ben many in other cuntres. . . . It is a good thing for a man that hath a good goshawke, or tercelle, or sparhawke for the perterich to have such houndes, and also when they byn taught to be crouchers they byn good for to take the perteriche and the quaile with a nette."

Hounds that hunt by scent had an irresistible attraction to our forerunners. Writers on Beagles like to think that these gay little hounds were here in the days of the Ancient Britons, and they quote Oppian, who wrote on hunting in the second century after Christ.

> There is a kind of dog of mighty fame
> For hunting, worthier of a fairer frame :
> By painted Britons, brave in war, they're bred,
> Are Beagles called, and to the chase are led.

We are on surer ground when we tell of Bloodhounds coming over with William the Conqueror. From his Abbey in the Ardennes, St. Hubert (d. A.D. 727), like so many other dignitaries of the Church, combined religion with sport, and his hounds acquired great fame, especially the black St. Huberts, progenitors of the Bloodhound. The Talbot, which from the twelfth to the sixteenth century was much in use in England, may either have

THE DUKE OF HAMILTON'S MASTIFF AND GREYHOUNDS
Oil painting by Sawrey Gilpin, 1780

sprung from the white St. Huberts or from one of the breeds of French hounds. It was a big, slowish hound, and there is little doubt that its blood survived in the big Staghounds which, until comparatively recent times, were hunted in the west country. The Shrewsbury family (Talbots) has two hounds as supporters to its coat of arms. Talbots may, too, have had something to do with the making of the old Southern Hound, a lightly-marked, bad-fronted, heavy hound with deep flews, long ears, and hanging dewlap. Shakespeare, whose knowledge of woodcraft is apparent in a number of his plays, may have had him in mind as he wrote those stirring lines in *Midsummer Night's Dream* :

> My hounds are bred out of the Spartan kind,
> So flewed, so sanded : and their heads are hung
> With ears that sweep away the morning dew;
> Crook-kneed, and dewlapped like Thessalian bulls.

(Here "sanded" means "flecked.")

By way of contrast, the Northern Hounds, also big, were more lightly built, and therefore faster, and not so strong in the head. In all probability an

15

amalgam of the two with some Greyhound thrown in to give speed, was the means of producing one of the most perfect of animals, the modern Foxhound. It is fairly easy to reconstruct a picture of the manner in which our forefathers enjoyed their field sports—coursing, hunting and hawking, in all of which dogs or hounds were employed. Present-day custom, by the way, restricts the use of the word "hound" to those that hunt by scent, Greyhounds and the like being dogs. I am unable to say when this convention first came in, except that in *The Master of Game*, the term "hound" seems to have been applied to Spaniels and others. Turbervile, however, in his *Booke of Hunting* (1576), refers to Greyhounds as "dogs."

In the eighteenth century the skill of Bloodhounds was tested in public. Here is an extract from the *Diary of a Gentleman of Fashion*, dated 1725 : "Monday S'enight went to Ranelagh, and following day went to Kennington Common, to see a tryal of bludhounds that are to be sent to the Low Countries to track Criminals. One dogge scented true, but the other was scarce so satisfactory. Saw numerous noblemen and people of fashion there, including the gentleman of quality I became acquainted with in the Park, and to whom I lost a wager of five guineas through the bludhound I favoured being so wrong in the nose."

Reading between the lines, we realise that in the early days of the Forest Laws dogs were kept by the populace that were too small to interfere with the game for the test applied was to ascertain if they could pass through a wire loop of standard dimensions. For some centuries it was not thought to be out of place to take dogs to church, notwithstanding the unseemly incidents that occurred. In parish records we read of small sums being paid to men whose duty it was to preserve order among the four-footed "worshippers," and churchwardens were equipped with dog nawpers that enabled them to deal with unruly tykes. After the destruction of rood screens at the Reformation it became necessary to separate the Sanctuary from the Choir by a rail, and in 1636 the Bishop of Norwich or Ely ordered that a rail be made before the Communion Table so thick with pillars that dogs could not get in, the reason for which may be inferred from a passage quoted by Stevens in his *History of Downing College :* "There happened in the town of Tadlow a very ill incident on Christmas Day 1638 by not having the Communion Table railed in. For on sermon time a dog came to the Table and took the loaf of bread prepared for the Holy Sacrament in his mouth and ran away with it."

Three centuries before that unhappy affair William of Wykeham reproved the nuns of Romsey : "We have convinced ourselves by clear proof that some of the nuns of your house bring with them to church birds, rabbits, hounds, and suchlike things, whereunto they give more heed than to the offices of the church." When William Warburton, Bishop of Gloucester, was in the Abbey Church at Bath one Sunday the first chapter of Ezekiel was read in which the word 'wheel' occurs several times. The sound was so reminiscent of hard labour to the Turnspits who were present with cooks that "they all clapt their Tails between their Legs and ran out of the Church." Before the invention of jacks, Turnspits—dogs with short crooked legs, long bodies and curly tails—were taught to turn the spit as a joint was being cooked.

As far as I am aware there is no evidence to show approximately the date at which small pet dogs were introduced into England, but, as a dainty Toy Spaniel was common to the Continent in the fifteenth and sixteenth centuries, it requires no effort of the imagination to picture some of them being brought here. Henry VIII decreed that no dogs should be kept in Court except "some small spanyells for ladies." They were then called spaniels gentle or comforters, the superstition being that one held to the breast would cure anyone of a disease. These little dogs appear in innumerable paintings, with pointed muzzles and long ears, and together with Italian Greyhounds they seem to have been the principal pets of the ladies until Pugs followed William and Mary from the Netherlands. Before this change of rulers occurred Charles II and James II became greatly attached to some of the Toy Spaniels, the descendants of which still bear the name of Charles. The Hon. Mrs. Neville Lytton (now Baroness Wentworth), in her comprehensive work on *Toy Dogs and their Ancestors*, quotes a passage from an old book to show one virtue of the little dogs : "The smaller ladyes popees that bear away the flees and dyvers small fowles." It is a novel idea to think of pet dogs trapping fleas and lice. James II was so fond of his dogs that when, as Duke of York, the ship in which he was journeying to Scotland ran on a sandbank off the East coast, he was more concerned with saving them than the passengers and crew.

We are much indebted to Professor G. M. Trevelyan for the pictures he gives in his various books of domestic life in this country. In *England under Queen Anne*, an intimate scene is reproduced. The Lady Wentworth of that period had a son—Lord Raby—who was British Ambassador in Berlin, to whom she wrote about the happenings in her home. In one letter she said : "I am sure could you see my fyer side, you would laugh hartely to see Fubs [the dog] upon a cushin, the cat of another, and Pug [the monkey] of another lapt up al but her face in a blanckitt." We do not know what kind of dog Fubs was, but, like so many of our pets, he came to a sad end, the cold winter of 1708 being too severe for him. "I had rather lost a hundred pound to have saved poor charming Fubs. As it leved soe it died, full of lov, leening its head in my bosom, never offered to snap at anybody in its horrid torter, but nussle its head to us and look earnestly upon me and Sue, whoe cryed for three days if it had been for child or husband . . . so much senc and good nature and not one falt; but few human creeturs had more senc than he had."

A general survey of the part played by dogs in British social life would be incomplete without a brief reference to the so-called "sports" of bull and bear-baiting, which went on from the Middle Ages until well into last century. That this brutal pastime gave pleasure to the spectators is obvious, but it does not seem to be certain that that was the primary object, the suggestion being that bulls, at least, were baited because it was supposed to make the flesh

17

tender. Was there a misreading of the original meaning of the word "bait"? In 1376 it was ordained at Cambridge that butchers should not sell the flesh of bulls unless they had been baited or fed with grass in a stall. Is it not possible that as time went on local authorities not learned in the law or orthography should construe the meaning as worrying by dogs? Anyhow, it became a well-established custom, and in 1591 the Privy Council forbade stage plays on Thursdays because they interfered with the "sport." It is almost inconceivable that as recently as 1802 attempts to prohibit bull-baiting should have been resisted in the House of Commons on the plea that it fostered pluck among the populace and encouraged manly exercises. It was put an end to in 1835, but dog fighting was permitted for some years longer.

Another diversion, less objectionable if no longer in conformity with modern taste, was that of matching dogs against one another to see which could kill the most rats, released in a pit, in the shortest time. We prefer now to hunt the rats with Terriers in their hiding places, and so perform a useful purpose by destroying these noxious vermin. S. C. Calverley, whose verses were more read in my young days than now, commemorated the custom in "*Hic Vir, Hic Est.*" He was describing the accomplishments acquired by undergraduates at Cambridge:

> Struck, at Brown's, the dashing hazard;
>   Or (more curious sport than that)
> Dropped, at Callaby's, the terrier
>   Down upon the prisoned rat.

Sometimes the dogs worked alone. There is a story of one, Billy by name, who killed 100 large rats in 6 min. 35 sec. In another match he reduced this time by 22 sec. In his old age, when he had but two teeth in his jaws and was minus one eye, the owner of a Berkshire bitch laid thirty sovereigns that she would beat the veteran. the number of rats being 50. Billy finished off his lot in 5 min. 6 sec., while the bitch fell exhausted after she had accounted for thirty.

In one respect our forebears made a practical use of dogs that is no longer followed by us although it is of considerable economic value to small tradesmen on the Continent. It was a common thing to see dogs pulling carts in the streets, and the custom was not finally prohibited until 1856. London, however, took the lead in 1839, when the police issued a notice to the effect that after January 1 of the following year "every person who within the Metropolitan police district shall use any dog for the purpose of drawing any cart or barrow shall be liable to a penalty of not more than 40s. for the first offence and not more than £5 for the second or any following offences." An attempt to make the embargo general came before the House of Commons in 1843, when a Mr. Barclay urged that it would be "an uncalled for and an unnecessary violation of the rights of a large class of humble traders by whom dogs were used. The parties using them for purposes of draught were gener-

PORTRAIT OF THE ARTIST WITH HIS FAVOURITE NEWFOUNDLAND
Oil painting by Ben Marshall, 1811

ally knife-grinders and hawkers of various small wares through the country and in towns; the aid of dogs was found very useful to bakers, butchers and other traders. The prohibition of this aid from dogs was not justified on the plea that so employing them was cruel."

Mr. H. R. P. Wyatt in *Fragments of Findon*, records : "Letters used to be drawn from Steyning to Storrington by a team of dogs. Canon Palmer, rector of Sullington (who died in 1931 at the age of 95) relates how he remembers seeing the teams lying at rest on the green at Storrington in the middle of the day." In a letter to *The Times* in 1936 Mr. W. H. Curtis stated that fish was taken from Southampton to London in small carts drawn by two or four dogs, the driver sitting with his legs on the shafts. In *Old West Surrey*, Miss Gertrude Jekyll mentioned that the dogs were usually Newfoundlands, of which a team of four would pull three or four hundredweights of fish. Mr. C. E. Hodson wrote in the same newspaper : "I have heard my father say that when he was a boy (1820–30) the travelling shows which visited the country fairs were drawn by long teams of dogs, and the dogs' feet suffered very much on the roads." There is a suspicion that the opposition to the employment of dogs was prompted less from humanitarian motives than from the desire to suppress a nuisance, the barking when the animals were engaged in their duties having disturbed the citizens.

COCKER SPANIELS
Coloured etching by G. Vernon Stokes

DOGS AT WORK

DOUBTLESS the primitive savage who first tamed a wolf cub and started the race of domestic dogs did so with the idea that it might be trained to kill edible animals and so make life easier. Luxury dogs, as household pets might be called, would not come until civilisation had advanced many stages and men gathered together in communities. So it comes about that sporting dogs have always figured conspicuously in our history. For centuries they were restricted to Spaniels and Greyhounds, then were added the hounds that hunt by scent, and, after the invention of the fowling-piece, which largely superseded falconry and trapping game birds in nets, the Setter was evolved from the Spaniels for the purpose of quartering the ground in advance of the guns, finding the lurking game, and indicating their presence by standing in the statuesque position known as pointing. In the days of the Plantagenets, Spaniels were of two kinds—those that flushed the game to the hawk, whence our Springers, and the others called "crouchers," that had

ENGLISH AND IRISH SETTERS
Coloured etching by G. Vernon Stokes

to drive the partridges or quails into the net. To do this they would have to
pause, and creep along belly to ground. From that action to pointing would
be a simple transition.

In the course of time three varieties of Setters were produced—the English,
Irish and Gordon, all of which are handsome in appearance, kindly in nature
and easily trained. An old friend of mine insisted that a thoughtful Providence
had sent the gundogs into the world to be of use to man. I preferred to look
at it in another way, suggesting that man had been endowed with an intelli-
gence that enabled him to mould animals to his advantage. Although the
Setters have certain features in common, each is distinctive apart from its
markings.

The English Setter perhaps owes its fame to Edward Laverack, on whose
tombstone in the Shropshire village of Ash one may read : "To the memory
of Edward Laverack; born Keswick, 1800; died at Broughall Cottage, 1877.
This monument is erected by admirers in England and America." That
others before him had been breeding with an aim to the perfection of these

dogs is apparent from his own words. Laverack bought Old Moll and Ponto as the foundation of his kennels in 1825, which, according to him, came of a strain pure for 35 years. Such a reputation did his dogs obtain that they were often called Laveracks. That he valued appearance as well as work may be inferred from the fact that he exhibited at the early shows of the Kennel Club, and even before. In the catalogues of the shows held at the Crystal Palace in 1871 and 1872 we see that he entered two dogs at each, with curiously contradictory statements. In the first, after giving the pedigree of the dogs, he added : "Descended from the pure blood (supposed to have at that period been pure for 35 years) of the late Rev. A. Harrison's, near Carlisle, who bred Old Moll and Ponto; consequently, Mr. Laverack having had this strain for more than 44 years, making a continuous strain of pure blood for at least 79 years. Guaranteed correct." In 1872 he stated : "This breed exhibitor has had for now half a century, and prior it was in the hands of the Rev. A. Harrison, near Carlisle, Cumberland, consequently has been kept pure for eighty-five years. Exhibitor guarantees this correct." Which was correct?

It is not of much significance beyond showing that Laverack was somewhat careless with his records. What we should like to know is how Mr. Harrison made his strain. The reasonable supposition seems to be that the English Setter is a developed Spaniel, bred larger by selective breeding. These dogs were often spoken of as Spaniels in the north until comparatively modern times. Chance references in some old authors suggest that a cross of Pointer had been introduced. If this were the case I can see no traces of it now. Sportsmen occasionally in the past crossed the two, calling the progeny Droppers, but the experiment did not seem to meet with much favour. When I mentioned this opinion in an article in the *Field* a correspondent wrote to say that his experience with such a cross was most satisfactory. Contemporary opinion differed concerning the merits of Laverack's dogs, the sum of the criticism being that when they were good they were very good, but when they were bad they were horrid.

Similar strictures did not apply to the strain started on pure Laverack blood by the late Mr. R. L. Purcel Llewellin, a Shropshire sportsman, who grafted on to it the best from other kennels, thus producing dogs beautiful in appearance and almost unexcelled in the field. They became popular in America as well as this country. The English Setter is handsome and kindly, and is invaluable in the field. Irish Setters are favourites with exhibitors and the public, who want companions rather than shooting dogs, perhaps because of the beauty of their rich golden chestnut colour. They were not always wholecoloured, white and red being common at one time. Perhaps they are a bit more headstrong than their English relatives, but when broken well they are all that the shooting man could desire, and latterly they have been running most successfully at field trials. How Setters of that particular colour came about is not known, but it may be that they sprang from a tall French Spaniel that had red markings.

POINTERS
Coloured etching by G. Vernon Stokes

The Gordon Setter, less Spaniel-like than the others, is also bigger and heavier. He is slower, too, at work, some would say less flashy, but he passes little game and is most persevering. The variety had sunk to about its lowest ebb in this country when about 1927 the British Gordon Setter Club was established for the furtherance of its interests. The black-and-tan dogs, however, had a firm footing in the U.S.A. as well as the Scandinavian countries. The father of the variety was the fourth Duke of Gordon, who died in 1827. Black-and-tan Setters were known as long ago as the seventeenth century, but it was this Duke's kennels that brought them into prominence. The story runs that the Duke once saw a shepherd's bitch that pointed grouse, and that by breeding from her he started the Gordons. Critics have declared that this was apocryphal, but the late Mr. Isaac Sharpe, who was interested in all gun-dogs, had heard the story confirmed by a head keeper in the employ of the ducal family.

The Pointer had a worthy historian in the late Mr. William Arkwright, whose fine work *The Pointer and his Predecessors*, is one of the best monographs on dogs that we have. He came to us ready made from Spain in the opening years of the eighteenth century, having probably been introduced by our soldiers after the Peace of Utrecht in 1713 released them from duty on the Continent. Smooth of coat and well balanced all through, he is a most attractive dog that does work identical with that of the Setters. Which you prefer is purely a matter of taste, each having its adherents. Old sportsmen, in the hope of improving a dog that was not really in need of any such process, introduced a cross with the Foxhound, which met with strong disapproval from Mr. Arkwright and others, who contended that it had the effect of making the dogs hunt with too low a head and gave the wrong formation of face. Arkwright insisted that the Pointer should be dish-faced—that is, have a concave muzzle, which was a sign of facility in scenting. "A Pointer carries head and neck outstretched in his gallop, and the higher the nose is presented to the wind the farther off it will perceive the body scent that is gradually rising from any neighbouring birds."

A century ago Pointers and Setters were entrusted with the duty of retrieving game when shot as well as finding it for the guns, and then it gradually began to occur to men that it would be more convenient to have what General Hutchinson in his classic work on *Dog Breaking* called a "regular retriever." Writing in 1847, however, he was not satisfied about the desirability of such auxiliaries. "We all have our prejudices," he said. "One of mine is to think a *regular* retriever positively not worth his keep to you for general shooting *if one of your setting dogs will retrieve well*—but what an all-important 'if' is this." None the less, he was of opinion that one was desirable for cover shooting provided he could be worked by signal in perfect silence. Hutchinson considered that the best retrievers were bred from a cross between the Setter and the Newfoundland or a strong Spaniel and the Newfoundland, adding : "I do not mean the heavy Labrador, whose weight and bulk is valued because it adds to his powers of draught . . . but the far slighter dog reared by the settlers on the coast." It was this smaller, smooth-coated dog that afterwards became known as the Labrador, some of which were brought back by fishermen.

These crosses between the Labrador and either a Spaniel or Setter gave us what are now Flat-coated Retrievers or Curly Retrievers, and until the opening years of this century they were in common use, the Flat-coat becoming the greater favourite. Fortunately, a few noble families, including the Duke of Buccleuch and Lord Malmesbury, preserved the Labrador, and in 1903 the Hon. A. Holland Hibbert, later Lord Knutsford, introduced them to a wider public by exhibiting at the Kennel Club show and running at field trials. This started a fashion that ended in Labradors largely supplanting the Flat-coats on the show bench and at trials. This is not the place in which to trace in detail the development of these wonderful retrievers that have figured so conspicuously at trials and in the show ring. Since 1914, Lorna Lady Howe has devoted herself to the encouragement of a dual-purpose Labrador—that

COURSING ON EPSOM RACECOURSE
Coloured engraving after S. N. Sartorius

G. VERNON STOKES

By courtesy of the Artist and M. C. Dickins, Esq.

LABRADOR RETRIEVER
Coloured etching by C. Vernon Stokes

is, one that can win at trials or shows. Many others have taken their share in the labour with unqualified success. Compactly built, with a broad skull, rounded otter tail, and short, hard coat, these dogs are distinctive. They may be black or yellow.

The Flat-coat is not so broad in skull, is constructed on beautiful lines and has a longish, flat coat with plenty of feathering. Although he has not appeared so much in public lately, he is still largely used by shooting men and game-keepers, his chief supporter for more than sixty years having been Mr. H. Reginald Cooke, who has now retired from showing and is confining himself to the breeding of utility dogs.

Of more recent introduction is the Golden Retriever, which was brought into prominence about 1908 by the late Lord Harcourt, then the Hon. Lulu Harcourt. Enquiries elicited that they were the descendants of dogs kept by the first Lord Tweedmouth in Scotland, and the story got about that this gentleman, then the Hon. Dudley Marjoribanks, bought his originals from a troupe of performing Russian dogs that he saw at Brighton soon after the Crimean war. About 1926 I asked Lord Tweedmouth, grandson of the gentleman in question, if he could confirm this belief. He could not, writing instead that "one Sunday, when my grandfather was at Brighton with my father in, I should think the late 'sixties, he saw a very good-looking yellow retriever, and approached the man with whom it was with a view of ascertaining its history, and where it had come from. It turned out that the man was a cobbler, who had received the dog in lieu of a bad debt from a keeper in the neighbourhood. It had apparently been the one yellow puppy in a litter of black wavy-coated retrievers. . . ." The upshot was that Lord Tweedmouth bought the dog and found a mate of the same colour in the Border country. It is only proper to say that Mrs. Charlesworth, who has been one of the keenest supporters of the variety, believes in the earlier story. Whichever may be correct, the dogs are much liked and have made considerable headway.

Curly Retrievers went much out of favour and were only preserved by exhibitors, who spent endless trouble in getting small tight curls all over the body. Since 1933 efforts have been made to revive them as workers as well as show dogs, in which one of the prime movers has been Brigadier-General F. F. Lance.

For the modest sportsman one of the members of the important Spaniel family is as useful as any. At one time they were classified roughly into land Spaniels and water Spaniels, but, as shows grew in numbers and influence, a more exact nomenclature was found to be necessary, and they are now divided into seven varieties, all of which are distinct. This did not occur until shows had been running for some years, and in the meantime they were bred more or less indiscriminately, the progeny being registered under the variety they most resembled. Shows usually provided classes for Field Spaniels under 25 lb. and over that weight, which was not very illuminating. Clumbers were always regarded as being different, and they preserved their identity. As for the rest, Cockers were the first to emerge from the ruck, having been given a separate classification at the Kennel Club in 1892. They had gone under that name previously, but there was nothing to prevent them being bred with English Springers. The Spaniel Club required that Cockers should not exceed 25 lb. in weight, but this being considered too arbitrary the limit was withdrawn in 1901, after which progress was uninterrupted, until at the time of writing they stand at the head of all breeds. They have improved considerably within my recollection, and at their best are delightful dogs. The fixation of the red or golden colour since the Great War of 1914–18 has been the means of enlarging the interest in them.

Perhaps the one-dog shooting man will agree that an English Springer is one of the handiest assistants that he could have, being large enough to retrieve with ease. A weight of about 40 lb. gives him plenty of strength in his symmetrical body. Although the range of colours is not quite as wide as that of the Cocker, it admits of enough variety to suit all tastes. The Welsh Springer, which is usually a bit smaller and has shorter ears, should uniformly be of a rich dark red colour on a white ground. The Sussex Spaniel is heavier in body, the weight going up to as much as 50 lb., shorter on leg and altogether more massive. There is no mistaking one on account of its characteristic rich golden-liver colour and heavyish head with beetling brows.

The modern Field Spaniel, a product of the showman's art, has undergone several metamorphoses. Once he was so long in body, short in leg, and heavy that he was not a deal of use to the shooting man. The subsequent reaction that set in brought about a taller, more active dog, which should be capable of performing the duties expected of his kind. I do not mind expressing my admiration of the Clumber Spaniel, which is certainly a handsome dog in his white coat with lemon markings. The head is impressive, the short legs are strong in bone, and he is heavier than the others. Altogether different, indeed, from the remainder of the Spaniel family. He is an excellent worker, as King George V appreciated when he added a team to his kennels at Sandringham to act as beaters. Little is known about the origin of the Clumbers save that the first in England are said to have been presented to the Duke of Newcastle, who lived at the end of the eighteenth century, by the Duc de Noailles.

The Irish Water Spaniel, again, has individuality. The crisp curls that cover the body, the dark rich liver-puce colour, the whip stern, and the length of leg place him in a class by himself. Whether he was the result of a cross between a red Setter and Poodle or is indigenous to Ireland is not sure.

All the gundogs have ample opportunities of showing their worth at field trials, many of which are held in the course of a season. The first of its kind took place at Southill in Bedfordshire in 1865, and the numbers gradually increased, but the greatest expansion took place after the Great War. The general effect has been to raise the working level of these dogs, to produce a degree of efficiency that was probably unknown to our great grandfathers, although dogs meant so much to them in their sports.

26

FOXHOUNDS RUNNING IN COVERT
Coloured engraving after R. B. Davis, 1833

HOUNDS THAT HUNT BY SCENT

ANY picture of the sporting life of Great Britain would be wholly incomplete without reference to the greatest of all sports—foxhunting. Yet it is by no means our earliest sport. Turbervile, whose *Booke of Hunting* was published in 1576, found small pastime in hunting the fox, but it may be that was the opinion of the French author whose work he translated. This, however, is his own : "Whereas in huntyng with houndes, although the pastyme be great, yet many tymes the toyle and payne is also great : And then it may well be called, eyther a paynefull pastyme, or a pleasant payne." Professor G. M. Trevelyan explains in *England under Queen Anne* how the tastes of country gentlemen came to change. He writes : "Foxhunting, like so may other English institutions under Queen Anne, was beginning to assume features recognisably modern. . . . The disorders of the Civil War had broken up deer-parks and destroyed deer to such an extent that at the Restoration the fox was perforce substituted in many districts. In the first decades of the eighteenth century there were no county or regional packs supported by public subscription, but private gentlemen kept their own packs and allowed their neighbours to follow." It is thought that the first pack to chase the fox exclusively was the Charlton in Sussex, that afterwards became the Goodwood.

The sport grew to such an extent that more than 200 packs have been kept for the purpose at a cost that must have run into several millions a year. John Jorrocks had his own ideas about hunting. "The sport of kings, the image of war without its guilt, and only twenty-five per cent. of its dangers." He also held that "the 'orse and the 'ound were made for each other, and natur' threw in the fox as a connectin' link between the two."

Hounds and horses have changed in a little over a century, both growing faster and the hounds having more thrust and drive. The Foxhound has for long been one of the most perfect animals in all the dog world. How he was fashioned is conjectural, the supposition being that the Talbot was the foundation and that Greyhound blood was invoked to give greater pace. The difference between the hounds of the fashionable packs and those with less pretensions is striking, and in the Fell country of Cumberland and Westmorland we have a different type—a more lightly-built hound with hare feet (rather than the round cat feet), which are more suitable for clambering up rocks and working in rough hills. Wales, too, has hounds of its own, mainly lightly marked and wiry of coat.

Harriers for hunting the hare are now chiefly nothing more than small Foxhounds, though in the West country and elsewhere we have some survivors of the genuine old English Harriers, often mottled, more leggy, not so powerfully built, but their noses are said to be excellent.

Beagles for hunting hare, which may be followed on foot if they are not too tall, are essentially English, and have furnished sport for kings and gentry for many generations. Forty or fifty years ago they used to be a feature of our principal shows, where Masters and followers gathered for gossip and criticism. In Ireland there are the Kerry Beagles, which are very dissimilar, being taller than many Foxhounds and black-and-tan in markings. Some of their supporters think they sprang from Bloodhounds, taken into the country by Irish officers who had served with the French armies.

Basset Hounds are other hare hunters, and most persevering they are with their wonderful noses. Short-legged, something of the Dachshund formation, they are much heavier than the badger dogs and are hound marked. In common with Beagles they were a feature of shows at the end of last century and beginning of this, and they, too, had their lapse. A few packs remain and there are hopes that they may increase in numbers.

The history of the Bloodhound is such that chapters might be written about him without exhausting the subject. Most of my readers will have read how they were employed in unsettled times on the Borders of England and Scotland for tracking marauders, and several centuries ago an impost was levied on a district for the cost of keeping Bloodhounds to trace sheep-stealers and other miscreants. If it had not been for shows they would probably have died

HARRIERS
Coloured engraving by Reeve after Dean Wolstenholme, senior, 1757–1837

out, but these kept them alive, and when the Association of Bloodhound Breeders was formed about 1898 a cardinal feature of their programme was the promotion of man-hunting trials. As a consequence, a few Chief Constables have used them for the detection of crime with excellent results. Bloodhounds are trained to hunt what is termed the "clean boot," or, in other words, to track a human runner whose boots have not been dressed with aniseed or any other concoction.

They should be so clever that if the line is crossed by a stranger they will not be diverted by the newer and hotter scent, and at the end of the chase they should be able to pick out the man they have been hunting although he may be concealed among a dozen others. It is this freedom from change that gives reasonable assurance to the police when a man whom they have not seen is caught. At least they feel justified in detaining him for further enquiries. Further, Bloodhounds can hunt a line much colder than any other hounds are capable of doing. Naturally, a good deal depends upon the scenting conditions of the moment, these being much more favourable in certain states of the atmosphere, as Masters of Foxhounds and owners of gundogs realise. Here is an example of what is possible. At 8 o'clock one morning a young school teacher in Gloucestershire set out on her bicycle for the school and was not seen again, but the machine was found at the entrance to an estate. The locality having been searched thoroughly without result, early the next morning the police called on Mrs. Michael Sadleir, an enthusiastic trainer, to ask if she would take one of her hounds. She could not go herself, being on the point of starting for a show, but she lent them a young hound, which was taken to the place where the bicycle had been left, and there encouraged to pick up the line. This he did so well that the body of the girl was discovered in a lake.

Bloodhounds are distinguished by their long narrow heads covered with a mass of wrinkles, and long, low-set ears and deep dewlap. Aristocratic in appearance, they are in disposition nature's gentlemen, seldom showing evidence of temper.

In a book designed to have a general appeal it is not necessary to give much space to the Otterhound for there are few of them, though records of the sport go back as far as the reigns of Henry II and his son King John. Whether Otterhounds come from the Southern Hound with crosses that gave them their rough coats, or one of the French hounds, is not certain. They have some resemblance to a Bloodhound with rough, wiry coats, and I should say that they are better for their work than the Foxhounds that constitute most of the packs.

THE DUKE OF CUMBERLAND'S DOGS
Detail from a water colour by Paul Sandby, 1725–1809

30

THE GREYHOUND FAMILY

A GREAT family this, that has been known from time immemorial. The most important of the lot from the British point of view is the Greyhound, to which reference has been made in the chapter on the Forest Laws. As coursing does not admit of any considerable variation it is not surprising to find Flavius Arrianus, better known by his pseudonym of Xenophon, writing in the first century of the Christian Era as one might write to-day. He would not have more than a brace of dogs in a course, and he urged giving the hare plenty of law before the dogs were slipped. Turbervile wrote an original chapter on coursing in his *Booke of Hunting*, from which we gather that in Tudor England Greyhounds were used on deer, hare and fox. In coursing the hare, the dog that killed was not necessarily the better, and so it is to-day. A number of coursing meetings are held every season, of which the principal is the Waterloo Cup promoted by the National Coursing Club. The late Lord Dewar once told me that he thought it almost more difficult to

"BRAN," A CELEBRATED SCOTTISH DEERHOUND
Oil painting by Thomas Duncan, 1807–1845

win the Waterloo Cup than the Derby because of the accidents that might occur to destroy the chances of a good dog. Greyhound racing, which now attracts many thousands of spectators, came to us from America about 1926. Show Greyhounds, being bred purely on account of their looks, are among the handsomest of dogs.

That there were huge wolf-dogs in Ireland from a very early date has been clearly established, and their value in the destruction of wolves was recognised by some of our monarchs centuries ago, the third Edward being one of them. They appeared in the arms of ancient Irish kings with the motto, "Gentle when stroked, fierce when provoked." One day in reading the *Love Letters of Dorothy Osborne* (1652–54) my attention was arrested by chance references to these dogs. Writing to her lover, Sir William Temple, she begs : "When your father goes into Ireland, lay your commands upon some of his servants to get you an Irish greyhound . . . Whomsoever it is that you employ, he will need no other instructions but to get the biggest he can meet with; 'tis all the beauty of those dogs, or of any, indeed, I think." She had hoped to receive one through Henry Cromwell, and later on two were given to her by him. By the time Goldsmith published his *Animated Nature* (about 1770),

32

LURCHER
Oil painting by Philip Reinagle, 1749–1833

they had become very rare. The largest he had seen was "about four feet high.
. . . He was made extremely like a Greyhound, but rather more robust."
Before accusing Goldsmith of exaggerating one would like to know how he
based his estimate. I have seen one that exceeded 37 in. at the shoulder,
which would have been close on 48 in. if measured to the top of the head.
Irish Wolfhounds had almost disappeared when the late Captain G. A.
Graham began to resuscitate them in 1862 by means of Deerhound blood.
Whether he succeeded in getting a faithful reproduction of the old breed or
not one cannot say. At least now we have a most imposing animal taking after
the Deerhound except for size.

It is not for me to discuss if Fingal lived and Ossian sang, if James Mac-
pherson was an impostor in claiming to have given us a translation of the
Ossianic poems. At least we may assume that his poems were based upon
tradition, if nothing more, and I like his picture of a thousand dogs flying off at
once, grey-bounding through the heath. Those dogs, of course, must have
been Scotland's famous Deerhounds, such as are still with us. They are
mixed up inextricably with Scottish history, the Chieftains having used them
first to course the deer, and later to track down animals that had been wounded

33

with the bullet. Now their chief avocation is to grace the show ring with their presence, and to serve as companions, but some that have gone to foreign lands have proved that the old hunting instinct is not dead but merely dormant from disuse.

It is possible that in the Saluki we have the latter-day representative of the forerunners of all the greyhounds, but one can say no more than that he is of very ancient derivation, probably having lived under the Pharaoh dynasty. He is the hunting dog of the Arabs, used for coursing gazelle or the desert hare, often in conjunction with a falcon, which, by striking at the head of the small antelope, impedes its progress. In the Mahommedan religion dogs are unclean except those that hunt, and any coming into the former category are often treated with cruelty, while great care is taken of the Saluki. Towards the beginning of this century the Hon. Florence Amherst became interested in these intriguing dogs, importing a few that were exhibited. At the close of the Great War, Brigadier-General F. F. Lance and others pushed them assiduously.

One assumes that the Afghan Hounds are close relatives of theirs, having diverged in certain essentials according to their environment. The Afghans themselves declare that their dogs came out of the Ark, but what is based merely upon tradition cannot be accepted as the truth without the evidence being subjected to close examination. It is easier to imagine that Salukis were taken by means of caravans into Persia and thence to Afghanistan, where they became modified by climate and the conditions under which they worked. Whatever is the explanation, we are left with a singular dog, and one that to me is rather fascinating. An American, setting eyes on one for the first time at one of the Kennel Club shows, remarked : "It isn't possible," and a girl at the same show declared that they looked moth-eaten. Both were wrong. But admittedly they look strange with hair on all four legs as if they wore trousers fore and aft, smooth backs and long hair under the body, heads with topknots, and long drooping ears well feathered. They have an innate dignity that separates them from the remaining dogs at a show, an Oriental aloofness, and the colour scheme of their coats is most attractive.

Borzois owe their standing in this country to the Duchess of Newcastle, who was stimulated to form a kennel towards the close of last century, after one had been given to her mother by a Spanish nobleman. In doing so she had the advantage of receiving advice from one of the Russian Grand Dukes, and so well did she follow her mentor and exercise her judgment that the breed was established on proper lines. That they are aristocrats of high degree is apparent from their elegance of form and demeanour. Tall, and covering much ground as they stand, they show that they are built for speed. In Imperialistic Russia they were the wolf-dogs of Tsars and Grand Dukes, some of whom kept up extensive establishments and hunted in great style. The customary method of hunting was for certain followers to take their stands at intervals round a wood, each holding three Borzois, and as a wolf was driven out of cover the dogs nearest to him were slipped. At other times dogs would be carried on troika sledges which followed the quarry until it became convenient to slip them.

Last of the dogs of this shape are Whippets, the poor man's Greyhound as they have been termed. They are actually Greyhounds in little, although when first made they came from a mixture of the bigger dog and probably Italian Greyhound or white English Terrier. They usually weigh up to 21 lb. Until Greyhound racing afforded a sport that was more spectacular and better organised, Whippet handicaps were popular in many parts of the country, and so great was the speed of these little sprinters that a good one could cover 200 yards in from 12 sec. to 15 sec. The competitors were trained to race to the rag, which means that as they were held on the mark their owners ran down the course waving a handkerchief or piece of cloth, at the same time yelling to excite the dogs.

AFGHAN HOUND
Wash drawing by B. Howitt-Lodge

35

OTHER SPORTING BREEDS

THE four remaining breeds that are classified as sporting are British only by adoption, all coming from abroad. Dachshunds, however, are so numerous and have been with us so long that we may well give them the privilege of naturalisation. Their first appearance was soon after Queen Victoria ascended the throne, several having been given to her by friends of the Prince Consort. Among the large number of pets that she had in the kennels at Windsor it is evident that they were favourites as may be gathered from inscriptions on stones erected to their memory. In the course of time more were imported from Germany and Austria, and we may justly claim to have had a large share in their popularisation. A club was formed here for their support ten years before a similar organisation appeared in Germany, and we also took precedence in exhibiting them. So indefatigable have British breeders been that they now take a high place among show dogs and they are common as companions. They belong to the meritorious army of workers, really being dual-purpose dogs. They will go to ground like terriers or track wounded game on the surface. The smooths have always been the most general, but the wire-haired and long-haired have their claims.

Occasional Elkhounds have been seen at shows for the best part of this century, but it was not until after the Great War that they won a definite place for themselves, thanks largely to the influence of Lady Halifax, then Lady Dorothy Wood, and Lieut.-Col. G. J. Scovell, who were instrumental in forming the British Elkhound Society. To ensure that we began with the type most approved Mr. W. F. Holmes made several journeys to Norway and Sweden, where he obtained the foundation stock for his kennels. These dogs, which are of the Spitz family, are trained to assist in the pursuit of that ungainly animal, the elk. There are two methods of hunting, in one of which the dogs are worked on a leash, while in the other they have their freedom. Those that work free show much cleverness in approaching the quarry. If they were too impetuous it would stampede; hence they advance cautiously so as to excite the curiosity of the creature without frightening it. Then by barking and feinting to attack they bring it to bay to give the hunters the opportunity of getting within shooting distance.

From the nearby land of the Finns has come a pleasing little sporting dog, also of the Spitz type, the cock-eared bird dog; otherwise, the Finnish Spitz. His job is to flush the big game birds that frequent the forests, follow them until they alight on trees, and then bark to apprise the guns of their whereabouts.

Now we have to make a mighty leap of thousands of miles into Central Africa to reach the habitat of the last dog in this chapter, which has arrived since the War of 1914-18. Not much larger than a Fox Terrier, with prick ears and curled tail, the Basenji, as we have named it, which means "Bush Thing," was discovered by Mrs. Burn when she was visiting her husband, who had

DACHSHUNDS
Pencil drawing by Vere Temple

an appointment on a tributary of the mighty Congo. She was so interested that she took several home with her, and afterwards received consignments by air. Mrs. Burn brought one for my inspection in the hope of getting some publicity for them, and in the course of our conversation she mentioned that they had one peculiarity—they did not bark. A note to the Press about the Barkless Dogs that were to make their debut at one of Cruft's shows excited so much interest that crowds assembled to have a look at these phenomena, and their position became assured.

37

THE TERRIERS

Britain would not be Britain to many of us without its terriers, those indefatigable, often noisy, sometimes gassy little rascals that assist in the destruction of vermin or occupy a place in the home with commendable adaptability. They exhibit a paradox that puzzles some. They may be expensive at a guinea or cheap at £1,000. The record price, I believe, was made by a wire Fox Terrier that was sold to America for upwards of £2,000. The explanation of such anomalies lies in the fact that, although thousands of indifferent ones may be bred, the really first-class specimens are not numerous. No doubt our great-grandfathers would be astonished at the number of distinct breeds and varieties that have been fashioned out of the rough since shows began in 1859.

In the grand total of 21 different sorts of terriers two only have come from overseas—the Australian and Boston, both of which, however, were manufactured from British material. What is more surprising, perhaps, is that nearly half remained in comparative obscurity until the opening of the present century, including West Highland White Terriers, Cairns, and Sealyhams. Staffordshire Bull Terriers, Kerry Blues, Norwich, Lakeland and Bostons did not come on the Kennel Club registers until after the resumption of shows in 1920. Before that the Bostons had enjoyed wide popularity in the United States, but no one here had been sufficiently enterprising to import them. The Staffordshires, too, had existed in the crude form of crosses between the Bulldog and terrier for more than a hundred years before they were bred long enough *inter se* to justify being registered as a separate variety. Camp, the product of such a cross, was Sir Walter Scott's prime favourite, and his passing so affected the great man that he cancelled an engagement to dine out on account of the death of an old friend.

Scott was so devoted to dogs that it is proper that Dandie Dinmonts should remain as a monument to the character of the Border farmer in *Guy Mannering*. Dandie Dinmont, this farmer, had the curious whim of naming all his hard-bitten terriers Mustard or Pepper, according to their colour. The public insisted upon regarding James Davidson of Hindlee as the prototype of this person, and they went to him for terriers of his breeding, though Scott had explained that he never met him until several years after the publication of the book. Dandie Dinmonts and Bedlingtons seem to have been closely allied in their beginnings, and Scotland has also given us others in Scottish Terriers—the foremost—West Highlands, Cairns and Skyes. England may well be proud of its Fox Terriers, smooth or wire, that have made a place for themselves in every part of the world. They came originally in response to the desire of Masters of Foxhounds to have terriers in which white predominated so that there could be no danger of hounds mistaking them for a fox as they came out of an earth. The probability is that Beagle blood was used to get the markings that are now characteristic. Norwich Terriers, which are

CUMBERLAND HUNT : HOUNDS AND LAKELAND TERRIER
Panel in oil by G. Vernon Stokes

not familiar to the general public, are small and sturdy, and are supposed to have come from crosses between Irish and Yorkshire Terriers.

Lakelands, once called Patterdale, are the terriers used to run with Foxhounds in the Lake country. Border Terriers, which hail from Northumberland, are rare little sportsmen with hearts as big as themselves. Bull Terriers are unexcelled for courage, having the pluck of the Bulldog combined with the dash of the terrier. Airedales, which were made in Yorkshire from the old black-and-tan terriers and most likely an Otterhound, are sensible and companionable. Wales may be well satisfied with Sealyhams and Welsh Terriers. The late Captain John Edwardes of Sealyham in Pembrokeshire, not being altogether satisfied with the terriers that were available, made an amalgam of several to produce the dog that has been named after his residence. The black-and-tan Welsh Terrier is presumably the survival of dogs that were at one time common throughout England. The old red Irish Terrier is a great dog that has fallen away from his high estate for no legitimate reason, and his rejuvenation would be welcome. The worst that can be said about the Kerry Blue (Irish Blue Terrier in Eire) is that his coat needs a deal of trimming if he is to remain presentable; otherwise, he is likable and distinctive.

39

THE NON-SPORTING BREEDS

TWENTY-SIX breeds and varieties appear in the non-sporting division of the Kennel Club, and here I cannot do more than indicate briefly a few of the features that give them a claim to interest. Having already dealt with Mastiffs in an earlier chapter I need say no more than that they are now of exceptional bulk, with heads that are shorter, more massive and more heavily wrinkled than those of a century ago or even less. Rivalling them in proportions are the St. Bernards, of which a stream of importations set in during the 1860's, the romantic story of their life-saving exploits on the Great St. Bernard Pass leading from Italy, having taken the public by storm. The most famous dog of those times was Tell, the property of the Rev. J. C. Macdona, but, judging by his pictures, he would compare unfavourably with his handsome successors, one of which was sold to America for £1,300. Newfoundlands, which preceded them by a good many years, were once esteemed greatly for their companionable qualities, and they are still as friendly and sensible as ever they were, but popular taste seems to have turned to dogs that are more active, such as Great Danes, large classes of which are to be seen at all the leading shows.

The handsome Collies, at their zenith towards the end of last century, have never since recaptured the glories of a period when they were making prices that seemed almost incredible. Border Collies have earned wider fame, not on account of their looks, but because they are beyond dispute the finest workers on sheep that we have. The Old English Sheepdog, sagacious and pleasing to the eye, would no doubt adorn more homes if people were not afraid of the labour involved in keeping his profuse coat in seemly condition. That good-natured, stolid, stout-hearted old friend the Bulldog remains as ever the embodiment of the British spirit. Long past are the days in which he was a sinister figure, and his appearance has changed considerably in the meantime. Fifty or sixty years ago a writer pleaded for the preservation of the Bulldog because of his usefulness in infusing courage into other breeds. He has done yeoman service in this direction, one of his most acceptable gifts being the Bullmastiff, which is a compromise in size between both his original parents.

The rise of the Alsatian immediately after the close of the Great War was unexampled, for so cleverly were his fortunes pushed by returning service men that for a short while he was at the head of all the breeds registered with the Kennel Club. In a sense he is sailing under false colours since he has no right to the name he bears. He should properly be the German Shepherd Dog, but, as with "silver" and measles, the word "German" as an adjective has not always been in favour. At his best, this dog is gifted with the quality of companionship to a high degree.

The first reference to Chow Chows of which I am aware is to be found in Gilbert White's eighteenth-century *Natural History of Selborne*, which has

COCKER SPANIEL
Oil painting by Maud Earl
By courtesy of the Leger Gallery, London

HOUND PUPPIES FEEDING
Chalk drawing by Vere Temple

its interest because the pair imported by a neighbour of his had two of the characteristics that still distinguish them—the black tongue and straight hocks. Why they should choose to flaunt a tongue of this colour is a matter that scientists have been unable to explain to me. After shows started again in 1920 they made much headway, and their progress was accelerated when the the late Mrs. Mannooch's Ch. Choonam Brilliantine was bought by Mrs. Earl Hoover of Chicago for £2,000.

Queer little dogs with foxy heads and short legs have for long been the cattle dogs of South Wales. About 1926 the Welsh Corgis entered upon a wider career, and the royal approval extended to them seven years later made their position among show breeds assured. The Gulliverian problem of Big Ends and Little Ends, in somewhat different form, at one time threatened trouble, but the Kennel Club ended the dispute by classifying the Pembroke and Cardigan as separate breeds, the former having short and the latter long tails. Get out of your minds the idea that Poodles are simply objects for ridicule because of the manner in which they are tricked out. They are among the cleverest of all, a fact that is a refutation of the belief that narrow heads imply stupidity. Something may be said, too, in defence of the old custom of barbering, which arose in the first instance because a full coat impeded the progress of the dogs when retrieving from water. It does show the shape of the dogs in all their pride and elegance. The miniatures, under 15 in., are charming little dogs.

We have to thank Mrs. Wingfield Digby, of Sherborne Castle, for the Keeshonds, with which she fell in love when she saw them on barges in Holland. They are similar in appearance to large Pomeranians without the range of colours common to that breed, and they are more sedate in manner.

A Collie in miniature, the Shetland Sheepdog is as smart as new paint, and for those who want a companion that is staid without being stupid there is the French Bulldog; Samoyeds, of the Spitz kind, with their stand-off white coats and pleasing manners, are really attractive. The Dalmatian at one time looked like making his departure from the stage, but now shows new vigour; Shih T'zu, brought from China by Lieut.-Gen. Sir Douglas Brownrigg and Lady Brownrigg, and several Tibetan breeds add an exotic touch, and there are others in this non-sporting division which might well be noticed.

THE DUKE OF CUMBERLAND'S DOGS
Detail from a water colour by Paul Sandby

41

MISS BOWLES AND HER SPANIEL
Oil painting by Sir Joshua Reynolds, 1775

THE LITTLE ONES

THE small pets classified as toys have had their ups and downs from the time of the old Greeks and Romans. Liking for these little creatures is no peculiar manifestation of modern days. One assumes that the first to come to us were the ancestors of the King Charles Spaniels, which were representatives of the pet spaniels that had a wide distribution throughout

WILLIAM HOGARTH WITH HIS DOG
Self portrait by Hogarth 1697–1764

the Continent. The great Marlborough had a variety which survives as the Blenheim, distinguished by its pearly white coat with chestnut red patches. The real King Charles is a black-and-tan, the tricolour has white added, and there is also the ruby, which is a whole-coloured chestnut red. Italian Greyhounds, delicate and fragile, and Maltese with their flowing white coats, were known in the reigns of the Stuarts. Pugs came from Holland with William and Mary, and these sufficed until about the 1870's, when Pomeranians were

43

imported from Germany. They were then principally white in colour and of a good size, but under the influence of shows exhibitors reduced the size and invented all sorts of charming colours.

The Pomeranian barometer was at set fair until with the opening of this century Pekinese came along to capture the imagination of exhibitors and general public as well. The rise of these dogs is rather remarkable. A few were picked up in the Summer Palace in Pekin when it was occupied in 1860, one going to Queen Victoria, and several passing into the Duke of Richmond's family, who continued to breed them. In the 1890's a few that were exhibited in classes for foreign dogs excited little attention, yet within six or seven years they became all the rage. They had been preceded by the Japanese, which at one time had promise, but the impression, erroneous to some extent, I believe, that they were delicate got about. More or less contemporary with them, too, were the Brussels Griffons, which have consolidated their position. Two British pets, Black-and-Tan Terriers (miniature) and Yorkshire Terriers, have their staunch admirers. Yorkies, when not too tiny, are sensible house-dogs. After 1920 we began to import Papillons, the forerunners of which are to be seen in numerous paintings and prints. With their large erect ears spread outwards they are supposed to resemble a butterfly with half-opened wings.

POODLE
Black chalk and pastel drawing by Lucy Dawson

44

ALSATIANS
Pencil drawing by Vere Temple

A NEW ERA IN DOGS

THE first dog show that ever was, held at Newcastle-on-Tyne in 1859, marked an important step, and may well be described as the opening of a new era. Not only did it lead to the improvement of the outward appearance of dogs, but it brought about the segregation of breeds, the discovery of new ones, and in the course of time it induced the public at large to pay more attention to the management and care of their domestic pets. The Newcastle effort was modest to a degree, competition being restricted to Pointers and Setters, of which there were sixty entries. Within a few months Birmingham followed with another, open this time to all the gundogs and a few other breeds, and before long the custom became general.

For some time the exhibits were accommodated on the floor of the building, which prompted one newspaper to write in 1860 : "It would have been well if the dogs could have been arranged on raised platforms, instead of lying on a level with the floor, as the space between them was not more than sufficient to accommodate one crinoline." Other times, other manners. The thousands of women and girls who now take part in these affairs often appear in breeches. Royal patronage was almost immediate, Queen Victoria and the Prince of Wales (afterwards King Edward VII) frequently exhibiting. A paper in 1865, describing a show in the Royal Agricultural Hall at Islington, remarked : "The Prince of Wales exhibited in several classes. If we may judge by the kind of dogs that H.R.H. sent we should suppose that he has a strong taste for manly exercises; thus, he had no Poodles, no fancy dogs of any kind. He had Greyhounds, and Deerhounds, and Mastiffs and Bloodhounds."

Before shows had been running many years practices that were, to put it mildly, undesirable, and in some cases simply fraudulent began to creep in, and it became evident that if decent people were to support the new sport there must be some sort of controlling body that had the power to warn off offenders and that would regulate shows. Thus it came about that the Kennel Club was founded in 1873 at the instance of the late Mr. S. E. Shirley, Warwickshire land owner and Member of Parliament. From the beginning the new body received influential support, and the Prince of Wales consented to become Patron. This honour was continued by him on his accession and since his death by all his successors on the throne.

One of the earliest acts of the new body was to introduce a system of registration as a condition precedent to exhibiting, under which on payment of a small fee, a dog received a distinctive name. For some years now it has been the rule that a registered name cannot be repeated in a breed for at least ten years.

For a while this wholesome system was only extended to shows held under the Rules of the Kennel Club, but about 1904 a rule was brought in enforcing universal registration. There was a great outcry from those who resented restraint in any form, but the public soon settled down under the new order, the acceptability of which was proved by the constantly increasing support accorded to shows.

This is not the place in which to explain the manifold ramifications of the Kennel Club, designed to regularise the manner in which shows shall be conducted, to prevent fraud and to preserve the purity of breeds. One effect may be stressed—that is, the multiplication of breeds and varieties. In 1873 the following 40 breeds and varieties were recognised :

SPORTING DOGS : Bloodhounds, Deerhounds, Greyhounds, Foxhounds, Otterhounds, Harriers, Beagles, Fox Terriers, Pointers, Setters (English), Setters (black-and-tan), Setters (Irish), Retrievers, Clumber Spaniels, Irish Water Spaniels, Spaniels (Field, Cocker and Sussex), Water Spaniels (other than Irish), Dachshunds (or German Badger Hounds).

BULLDOG
Water colour by B. Howitt-Lodge

NON-SPORTING DOGS : Mastiffs, St. Bernards (Rough and smooth), New-foundlands, Dalmatians (or carriage dogs), Bulldogs, Bull Terriers (all sizes) Sheepdogs and Scotch Collies, Black-and-Tan Terriers (except toys), Dandie Dinmonts, Bedlington Terriers, Skye Terriers, Wire-haired Terriers and Irish Terriers, English and other Smooth-haired Terriers, Broken-haired Scotch and Yorkshire Terriers, Pomeranians, Italian Greyhounds, Pugs Maltese, Blenheim Spaniels, King Charles Spaniels, Toy Terriers, Toy Terriers (smooth-coated), Toy Terriers (rough and broken-haired).

By 1905 the numbers had increased to 51, and the sub-divisions had become more logical, terriers, with the exception of Bull Terriers and White English Terriers (now defunct), being transferred to the sporting division. Since then the total has expanded to the following :

BREEDS RECOGNISED BY THE KENNEL CLUB

SPORTING

AFGHAN HOUNDS*	DACHSHUNDS,	FOXHOUNDS
BASENJIS†	LONG-HAIRED †	GREYHOUNDS
BASSET HOUNDS	SMOOTH-HAIRED	HARRIERS
BEAGLES	WIRE-HAIRED†	IRISH WOLFHOUNDS
BLOODHOUNDS	DEERHOUNDS	OTTERHOUNDS
BORZOIS	ELKHOUNDS*	WHIPPETS
	FINNISH SPITZ†	SALUKIS*

47

GUNDOGS

English Setters
Gordon Setters
Irish Setters
Pointers
Retrievers, ·
  Curly-coated
  Flat-coated
  Golden*

Retrievers,
  Labrador*
  Interbred
  Crossbred
Spaniels,
  Clumber
  Cocker

Spaniels,
  Field
  Irish Water
  Springer, English
  Springer, Welsh
  Sussex
  Interbred
  Crossbred

TERRIERS

Airedale Terriers
Australian Terriers
Bedlington Terriers
Border Terriers
Bull Terriers
  Miniature†
Cairn Terriers
Dandie Dinmont Terriers

Fox Terriers,
  Smooth
  Wire
Irish Terriers
Kerry Blue Terriers†
Lakeland Terriers†
Manchester Terriers
Norwich Terriers†

Scottish Terriers
Sealyham Terriers*
Skye Terriers
Staffordshire Bull
  Terriers†
Welsh Terriers
West Highland White
  Terriers*

NON-SPORTING

Alsatians, German Shep-
  herd Dogs†
Boston Terriers†
Boxers†
Bulldogs
Bullmastiffs†
Chow Chows
Collies,
  Rough
  Smooth

Dalmatians
French Bulldogs
Great Danes
Keeshonden†
Mastiffs
Newfoundlands
Old English Sheepdogs
Poodles
  Miniature (under 15 in.)
St. Bernards

Samoyeds
Schipperkes
Shih T'zus†
Schnauzers†
  Miniature†
Shetland Sheepdogs
Tibetan Terriers†
Welsh Corgis,†
  Cardigan
  Pembroke†

TOYS

Black-and-Tan Terriers,
  (Miniature)
Griffons Bruxellois
Italian Greyhounds
Japanese

King Charles Spaniels
Cavalier Spaniels†
Maltese
Papillons†

Pekingese
Pomeranians
Pugs
Yorkshire Terriers

* Admitted to the Kennel Club registers as a distinct breed or variety between 1900 and 1914
† Admitted to the Kennel Club registers since 1920

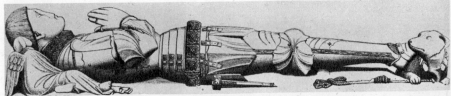

Monument to Robert, Lord Hungerford, d. 1455, in Salisbury Cathedral